# Self-Discipline:

## Techniques That Help Develop Willpower and Motivation to Live a Successful Life

# DISCLAIMER

Copyright © 2017

All Rights Reserved

No part of this book can be transmitted or reproduced in any form including print, electronic, photocopying, scanning, mechanical, or recording without prior written permission from the author.

While the author has taken the utmost effort to ensure the accuracy of the written content, all readers are advised to follow information mentioned herein at their own risk. The author cannot be held responsible for any personal or commercial damage caused by information. All readers are encouraged to seek professional advice when needed.

## Table of Contents

Self-Discipline: .................................................................................. 1

Techniques That Help Develop Willpower and Motivation to Live a Successful Life. ............................................................................... 1

Introduction .................................................................................. 6

Chapter 1: Cognitive Principles (Reason for Bad and Good Behavior)... 8

Chapter 2: The Habit Loop ........................................................... 12

    Empowered By Habits ............................................................. 14

Chapter 3: How to Replace Habits in the Habit Loop .................... 18

    Breaking Bad Habits .............................................................. 19

    Forming New Habits ............................................................... 19

        Identify ............................................................................. 20

        Experiment ....................................................................... 20

        Isolate .............................................................................. 21

        Plan .................................................................................. 22

        Making Them Stick ........................................................... 22

Chapter 4: The Power of Delayed Gratification ............................ 25

Chapter 5: Understanding the Psychology of Procrastination............... 27

    Ways You Can Stop Yourself From Procrastinating:......................... 31

        Step by step plan................................................................................ 31

        Being Realistic ................................................................................... 31

        Get Going............................................................................................ 32

        Taking Scheduled Breaks ................................................................. 32

Chapter 6: How to Be More Productive ..................................................... 33

Chapter 7: Utilizing Habit Pyramids .......................................................... 36

Chapter 8: Example - Utilization of Habit Pyramids on Fitness ........... 39

Chapter 9: Areas That You Can Apply Positive Habits. ......................... 42

Conclusion........................................................................................................ 46

# Introduction

There is every chance that your life is a total mess and you have no idea how it got so bad. If you are looking for a way to fix this mess, then you are in the right spot. What you should understand is that you are the only one with the power to fix this mess. So how can you start?

Understanding that you have no control at this moment over your impulses, your inner demons is the first step to take. Once you accept this fact you are ready to wrestle these demons into place. Understand that you will need to be stern with yourself when you get into situations where these demons are likely to emerge. These can be times when you are going to eat a second or third helping of food. They can be all those times when you know you should start working, but you put it off to do something more interesting - like talking with a colleague.

Here your demons will tell you that you should start the project tomorrow so that you can have a clean slate and have everything ready for a perfect job. It's at these times that you will need to squash these demons. When these demons tell you to start something tomorrow, you need to say "I am doing this now!" You will have to follow through. Otherwise your inner demons will have won. When you need to start a project, and your demons whisper to you to look for perfection, you need to say "I will start the project and finish it fully to the best of my ability!"

This starting and finishing of a task are an act which will help you maintain a level of self-discipline. Once you have these demons wrestled into control the next phase of being in control of your life is to make sure that you continue to act in these areas. As time goes by you will find that you have mastered these demons. You are now ready to face the next challenge in your life.

This is making maximum use of your time. You might ask what time has to do with getting your life on track. Well, if you look at the time you waste in any given day you will see there are huge chunks of time that you can use. These can be used to learn a new skill such as a foreign language or how to work a complicated computer program. These skills you learn will be of help to you later on in life.

Time management is an area where your total self-control and willpower are needed. As there are a number of distractions going on in life, you need to find a way to tune these distractions out. With these self-discipline techniques, you will learn to be aware of what is occurring in your life, but you won't let these events take over.

**Thanks for downloading this book. It's my firm belief that it will provide you with all the answers to your questions.**

# Chapter 1: Cognitive Principles (Reason for Bad and Good Behavior)

One of the basic principles of modern life is the maintenance of good relations between people and the desire to avoid conflict. This means that you can win respect and attention only if you are courteous and compassionate. But in life we often find ourselves confronted with rudeness, harshness, and disrespect. The reason here is that we underestimate the impact of human behavior and its mannerisms.

Manners constitute a way to behave, the external form of behavior and treating people. For speech, this constitutes expression, tone, intonation, body language, gestures and even facial expressions.

In a society, good manners are considered important. Self-discipline is considered the ability to control oneself and carefully and tactfully communicate with other people. Bad manners are considered to be the habit of speaking aloud, disregarding cultural gestures and behavior, carelessness in dress, rudeness, frank malevolence of others, disregard of other people's interests and needs, imposing oneself on other people's wills and desires, in the inability to control anger with the intention of insulting the dignity of the people around you, lack of tact, foul language, use of derogatory nicknames.

Manners are related to the culture of human behavior and are regulated by etiquette. Etiquette implies sympathy and respect for all people, regardless of their position or social status. It includes the courteous treatment of women, respect for elders, forms of address to the elderly, forms of address and greetings, rules of conversation, table manners. In general, etiquette in a civilized society coincides with the general requirements of courtesy, which are based on the principles of humanism.

Compassion is an obligatory condition of communication. Sensitivity should not be excessive or turned into flattery that could lead to unwarranted praise for anything seen or heard. There is no need to strenuously deny that it is the first time you have seen something, listened, eaten, or feared because otherwise, you will be seen as an ignoramus.

We are now living in an age where the meaning or implication of discipline is changing from what this word used to mean. I would like to know the response of the readers about the third interpretation of discipline given above. I guess that people (at least a good number) will disagree with or try to modify the word 'penalize' or 'punish.' Many experts believe and teach that punishment is wrong or unnecessary.

Let us turn to an illustration. In a competition, the athletes have to abide by the rules and regulations. An athlete does not become entitled to the prize even if he finishes the race fastest unless he keeps to the track assigned to him (II Tim 2). If he fails to follow the rules we declare that 'he made a foul' or that 'he is disqualified.'

Thus discipline involves some aspects. They are as follows:

(1) **Training and correction:** Discipline cannot be found overnight. It is established through training and practice. Any training involves correction and improvement. Discipline clearly requires practicing a principle over a fairly good period until one becomes sure that it flows from him naturally as and when it is expected of him.

(2) **Operating under rules, regulations, stipulations or norms:** Discipline also involves abiding by the rules framed by an organization or authority. So long as a person acts for or on behalf of an organization or body, he is governed by the rules/norms framed by that body. But what about things a person has to do independently, not as part of any organization? Who frames rules for his personal life? He has to frame norms or regulations for himself. He is the sole authority of his personality/self. He is responsible for things that happen in his life. For example, a student himself has to decide whether to study or not, how sincerely he should study, when he should wake up, and so on.

Discipline in personal life is governed by norms set by a person himself. However, since we are part of society, we are directly or indirectly indebted/responsible or answerable to people around us. I am talking about situations where a person has to act according to his conscience. This is where self-discipline or self-control plays a vital role.

(3) **Being aware of the rules:** Ignorance is not an excuse to being exempted from punishment. Can we afford to board a

plane or train and say we didn't know we had to buy tickets? Can we walk into class at 10.30 am and tell the teacher "I did not know the college starts at 9 o'clock?" Isn't that irresponsible behavior or indiscipline?

(4) **Obeying the rules:** When we already have set of norms, we should follow them. Ignoring rules, treating them passively or taking things for granted, not keeping to time frames, not attending to one's duties or being lazy and expecting someone else to take care of it and so on are classic examples of indiscipline. The spiritual world is particularly rampant with such inadequacies.

(5) **Having an aim/mission/purpose:** Most of the time, I feel, we are not purpose-driven, or maybe we do not pursue our mission with due zeal or determination. How serious are you about the purpose or goal? How pressing is the need to attain the goal. Discipline stems from an urgency of purpose and a clear vision. When we are focused, discipline follows naturally. Do we lack motivation or is it that we lack the grit to go through all the troubles and trials that accompany us? Whatever be it discipline is not devoid of trouble or pain. But let's just think for a while - who is it that is crowned with the title? Who is proclaimed as successful? It is the one who stands through all the thick and thin. That's the reward of discipline and perseverance.

# Chapter 2: The Habit Loop

Habits ultimately determine your destiny. More recent studies have even shown that habits, the act of conducting a task over and over again, may even affect our brain physically. Few of us are aware of our habits, how they are formed and how to create or break them.

In this chapter, I'll explain how the brain forms a habit, how you can break old ones and how to create new ones. Let's get started.

The most accepted hypothesis on how our brain works today is called "Hebbian Learning." The first principle of Hebbian Learning is that neurons fire together, wired together by creating what is called "synapses." The second principle is that the more these neurons fire together, the stronger the synapses become.

As synapses become strong, the firing of one neuron will result in the firing on those in its network.

Let's take walking as an example. A toddler wobbles when learning how to walk. His actions seem exaggerated, and he looks as if ready to fall anytime soon. This is because the neurons responsible for walking have not wired together as strongly as is needed to walk like an adult.

Once those synapses are formed, the behavior is formed. Thus, moving forward is an unconscious effort for most of us. You don't need to consciously think of which leg to put forward and which hand to swing.

In a way, you've just formed a habit.

The same principle applies to any habit. Some teenagers watch porn on a daily basis and thus form strong synapses that link porn to sexual gratification. When this happens, meaningful relationships and monogamy appear boring and no longer satisfy him/her.

Another common "addiction" is stress. Yes, most of us are addicted to stress and being busy. Here, try this: Sit down, close your eyes and meditate for 30 minutes. Think of nothing. Most of us couldn't focus on one task at a time, preferring instead to multitask, let alone sit and think of nothing.

This is why meditation is so difficult for most people - because we've formed a habit to be busy. Our mind constantly wanders - even when we are asleep.

By living in a sort of "addiction" and because habits are mostly unconscious, you're depriving the neurons in your frontal lobe, the part of your brain where your consciousness resides, of the opportunity to fire.

This leads to a variety of cognitive declines - such as the ability to learn. Because the flip side of the Hebbian Learning coin is that neurons that no longer fire together, no longer wire together.

As a toddler, we were able to walk because we practiced. But as we move into classrooms and offices, you spend less and less time walking, resulting in the inability to walk and balance in many older people. This is true even if they are physiologically able to walk.

To break a habit, you must first realize why your brain creates synapses. The point of the synapses is to make whatever tasks that you often engage in more effective (use less energy to achieve the same result). When it becomes more effective, it becomes easier, and so we choose to do it again - thus creating a loop.

So how can we break a habit? Make the habit undesirable (in other words, less effective)! You can do this by actively overriding a reactive decision (thus weakening a habit's synapse).

Another way is to make the reactive decision undesirable. For example, make a deal with your spouse that if you don't wake up early every morning and go for a jog, you'll help him/her wash the dishes for a week for every day you laze around.

Neurons responsible for lazing will then be associated with pain and de-associated with pleasure - thus breaking a habit.

## Empowered By Habits

Why do you do what you do? You have probably randomly stopped to ponder this question. You go through your day via habits: After waking up, you brush your teeth without thinking, and you stop at the same coffee shop for your morning cup every morning. If for any reason, you are not able to perform your habit that morning; your whole day seems off. This book discusses not only the power such daily habits have over you but, more importantly, how you can take control and use the power of habits to your benefit.

Habits are indeed powerful. Not only are you affected by the habits you (as an individual) have created for yourself but you are also strongly influenced by the habits of the organizations and societies you associate with.

As an individual, your brain is trained to follow something called the habit loop. The first step of a habit loop is a cue, a trigger that causes your brain to engage its' autopilot in steering you through your habit. The prompted routine (the second step) can be physical, mental or emotional. The last step of the loop is the reward. With time and practice, this loop becomes more and more automatic. The cue and the reward become intertwined creating a powerful sense of anticipation and craving. Eventually, a habit is born.

It is easy to imagine that certain habits are good and healthy while some others are less desirable. For example, sometimes boredom could be a cue to start drinking alcoholic beverages as time might seem to pass quicker (reward) while being a little tipsy. Or, the feeling of tiredness in the afternoon in your office might act as a cue for you to walk to the cafeteria to have a cookie or a bag of chips. In the latter case, you might be gaining weight which makes the habit undesirable for you at that moment.

Once you have an understanding of the cue-routine-reward cycle, you can start using it to your advantage by modifying any undesired habits you might currently have. The first step is to decide which habit you would like to modify. The second step is to gain awareness of what your cue, routine, and reward for that specific habit are. Once you are aware of your cue, you can consciously experiment with different, more desirable routines and observe if any of them brings you a similar reward or satisfaction. The more often the new chosen routine is repeated, the more automated the process becomes and a new habit is formed.

The book discusses the process of modifying the habits of individuals, organizations, and societies. The process in all three cases is very similar to the case of an individual discussed in the previous paragraph. The real-life examples are intriguing reading, while the practical approach provides a direct-action plan to tackle any undesired habits you might have.

It seems that you might start reading this book out of curiosity: 'Why do we do what we do in life and business?' You finish, however, with 'Let me decide now what I want to do in life and business as now I know the steps on how to form the habits that allow me to be my best.'

This book is a powerful tool to awaken your awareness of what habits are and how to use them to your advantage. Although the practical approach outlines a clear action plan to obtain your goals, it seems the reader is left to go through the process unsupported. For many, this process could benefit from an unconditional support from a great friend, discussion group or a life coach.

# Chapter 3: How to Replace Habits in the Habit Loop

Habits are the brain's way of engaging autopilot so that we don't have to consciously process all the amazing quantity of information it is receiving. We live in the information age, but our brain always has dealt with the constant flow of stimuli it gets when we are conscious has been a full-time job for it since we were conceived.

Some of these habits we will have deliberately developed - any learning for things we regularly do will eventually become a habit. You might put in extra thought-effort if you want either of these to produce a particularly neat result but the actions themselves should come automatically. This is good because it allows your brain to focus on other details instead.

Of the habits within us, some came without our conscious choice. This does not make them wrong. For example, our nose's sneeze response to pepper, or our stomach vomiting out 'poisons,' are good habits to rid the body of things that won't help. Likewise, the decision to put on one shoe before the other, cross your arms left-over-right (or vice versa) or to push with your calf when stepping forwards are all things you 'just do.'

This is obviously a basic belief, without which you need read no further. If habits can't be changed then we could never become better; people would never give up smoking, violent offenders could never be rehabilitated, and the whole personal development industry would grind to an abrupt halt! While some of these outcomes might be more desirable for you than others, it should be easy to accept that people's habits can be changed. The key to your success though, is to believe that you can change your habits.

## Breaking Bad Habits

The bad news first is that habits cannot be eradicated. They can be changed, though, and the change will overwrite the new to the point where, although your brain has the same old urges, your self-discipline allows the more recently formed to take precedence.

You need therefore to find a new routine to put in place when you notice the cue. You will then get the same sense of satisfaction, and your brain will be fooled into thinking that everything has carried on as before.

## Forming New Habits

Do you love what you do every day? If the answer is no, what are you going to do about it? I mean, what are you going to do about it?

Steps to breaking habits: identify it, experiment with rewards, isolate the cue and then have a plan.

**Identify**

What is it that you currently do that you would rather avoid? For me, it was the need to wander to the biscuit tin every hour or so when I was working at home. For you it might be drumming your hands in meetings, chewing the end of your pen or never putting the top back on the toothpaste. Whatever it is, knowing what you do is the start.

**Experiment**

Brainstorm possible benefits you might gain from your habit - remember that for your brain to keep urging you to do something it must know that you are getting something from this activity.

The next time you notice the urge to carry out the routine, do something different that might help to provide one of the possible rewards you might be aiming to provide for yourself. It could be anything, so long as it is not what you would normally have done. For example, you could tap your feet instead of drumming your hands, massage your scalp, cross your legs, stand up and turn around. The whole idea is to find something that still gives the reward you were craving when the urge kicked in.

For me, I tried making a coffee instead of eating, but that didn't work. I still had the urge to go for a biscuit. I walked around the house to distract myself, but that was similarly futile.

One way this book suggests, to work out what reward you need to satisfy you, is to make a few notes each time you do something different. After you have tried the experimental new routine, write three words or phrases down - nothing specific necessarily, just the first things that come to mind. It might be about your feelings or not. However, the moment of awareness does tend to focus you, plus it helps you recall your feelings later. Then set a 15 minute alarm; when it rings, ask yourself if the urge has been satisfied. If it has, what does this new routine also achieve for you, in common with the old habit? Obviously, if you still have the urge, then you will need to find a different alternative routine to provide the required reward. For me, I finally nailed it down as something to do with the joy of 'illicit snacking' - being able to take advantage of being at home for work. Only eating something met that 'need.'

## Isolate

If you can work out what triggers the urge, then you can start to make a plan. It will probably come from one of five areas: time, location, emotional state, other people or a preceding action. To isolate the cue, ask yourself a set of questions whenever you get the urge, along with the lines of the five themes, and note the answers. After a while, you should start to notice a common thread in answer to one of the questions e.g. it happens around the same time each day or in the same place, in response to a particular feeling or person or following a specific action by yourself or someone else. With me and the biscuits, I realized it happened every time I got up from my desk for any reason. I would amble into the kitchen and open the biscuit tin even if, for example, my original plan had been to collect something from the bookshelf.

## Plan

Once you have looked at the cue, the routine and the reward then you can make a plan. Expect the cue and when you get it recognize the urge and follow it by completing your new routine. The first time you do this will take mental effort to deliberately follow the plan. In fact, for the first few times, it will need you to be quite focused. Having some reminder will help you to recognize the cue instantly. If the cue is a time, then you can simply set the alarm, or if the location is key then a picture or sign in that place will jog your memory. If the cue comes from any of the other three areas, then it will not be as simple, but a life coach can help you associate the idea of your new with a memory of the cue.

One other alternative would be to disrupt the cue as you form a new habit. For example, if your habit is associated with the place then you could go somewhere else to get started. Looking back I can see how this unintentionally works for me nibbling at my fingernails, something I often did when driving long distances. I took a decision to stop one day early in a two week holiday. I didn't drive for a fortnight, and by the time I went home, I was well on the way to cementing the new habit. I have barely looked back since then.

## Making Them Stick

There are a few things that will help you make the new habit stick in the longer term.

1. Patience and Perseverance

You need some patience because it does not happen overnight. There is a popularly held myth that if you carry on religiously for 21 days, then that will be enough. It seems this originated from early plastic surgery patients who took three weeks to recognize their new faces. During this time it is possible, though not guaranteed, that you might fail, miss a day, or forget. If this does happen, you have a choice to either berate yourself for having fallen off the wagon or congratulate yourself for having lasted this long. As soon as you can, go back to your new habit, maybe reverting to the reminders you had in the early days to ensure it happens the way you wanted.

If you want the change badly enough though, you will stick to your plan and persevere through the harder days until the habit is ingrained, at which point persevering will be unnecessary - it will be habitual!

2. Belief

You need to believe that change is possible and that it is possible for you. It seems that it isn't necessary to believe in God or some other higher power but belief in the possibility of change is vital. Researchers have also discovered that within a group setting this belief is strengthened, even if that group is small. As you work on changing your habit, who will you share that with; who could support you as you develop yourself?

3. Craving

If you can turn your need to be rewarded into a craving, akin to an addiction maybe, then you are most likely to see the transformation that you desire. It's easy to see how this works with narcotics, but it is also possible with more good habits. When the cue triggers not only the routine but also the craving for the reward, then you will be highly motivated to ensure that the routine takes place faultlessly.

### 4. Support

Getting help from a friend or family member is always good whenever you want to develop yourself. They can encourage you, maybe put things in place around the edges that help and maybe most importantly, will keep asking how you are getting on. While it might grate occasionally, if someone external is providing a constant reminder of your goal then you will keep on going.

If you haven't got someone you want to confide in at home then it is worth considering employing a coach to help you through this stage of your growth - it's what they specialize in, and they can provide helpful tips and suggestions that make it all work well.

Changes can and must be made to our habits. By recognizing them, realizing what reward we are seeking and isolating what starts the process each time, we can make a plan to do something different. When this kicks in each time the urge takes us, we can still gain our rewards but through doing something which is more acceptable.

# Chapter 4: The Power of Delayed Gratification

Many of us were all too happy to use this cheap credit to purchase high priced items from jewelry, to clothes, to cars, to homes that are now coming back to bite us in the you know what. The consequences for American's lack of financial discipline over the past decade have led the world into a global financial crisis, which it is just recovering from. But, there is a silver lining in all of this. What could it be you ask? Well, this crisis gives us all the opportunity to take some time out and examine our spending habits and how these habits helped get us where we are today. I believe that now is as good a time as any to begin developing our financial leadership.

Now, let's be real, we can blame the banks for giving out cheap credit.

We can blame the federal government for encouraging the banks to give out more home loans to subprime borrowers.

We can blame one another for buying things we knew a bit out of our range.

However, we must still look inward to begin to explore and understand our contribution to the financial crisis America was in.

Your personal finances are more personal than financial. It is about properly allocating your financial resources (e.g. money) to be spent wisely- not emotionally.

Restraint is defined as the act or process of holding back or hindering from an action.

Restraint is about thinking first before spending. Restraint is your "personal finance due process" system. Restraint makes you ask yourself- "Do I need this?" It is not about being a cheapskate or misery. Instead, it is about carefully using your money they way you want it.

Now, when you acquire the habit of restraint in your personal finances, you will start to use it in cash in all your transactions. There is a stronger emotional attachment towards cash than credit cards. You are less likely to freely buy something with cash since you have a limited supply in your purse or wallet. That is where the principle or habit of restraint works in your favor. When you use a credit card, you just have them slide your card, and you sign something. It is much too convenient. More importantly, there is little or no restraint when using your credit card. You may use your debit card, but personally, I prefer to use cash for all transactions (e.g. groceries, gas, etc.).

Naturally, you will pay by writing a check or electronically transfer payments on your bills (e.g. electric, gas, water, etc.). On your day-to-day activities, you should use cash.

This is a good time to start to incorporate the principle of restraint in your favor. Later, you will be able to gain the benefits of restraint by acquiring the disciple of delayed gratification- which is a higher level of restraint.

Ask yourself:

How have I contributed to my financial crisis?

What questionable financial decisions have I made? And what can I learn from these decisions?

Be clear, if we don't explore this issue from an inside-out vantage point, we are doomed to fall back into this destructive pattern again.

The biggest and most penetrating question that you have to ask yourself is: Can I truly afford my lifestyle?

## A Short message from the Author:

Hey, are you enjoying the book? I'd love to hear your thoughts!

Many readers do not know how hard reviews are to come by, and how much they help an author.

I would be incredibly thankful if you could take just 60 seconds to write a brief review on Amazon, even if it's just a few sentences!

Please head to the product page, and leave a review as shown below.

Thank you for taking the time to share your thoughts!

Your review will genuinely make a difference for me and help gain exposure for my work.

# Chapter 5: Understanding the Psychology of Procrastination

Being a procrastinator is not something that we desire, and yet most of us are! Procrastination is the single most nonproductive skill that we have mastered well because it is a vicious cycle that feeds on us giving it momentum every time we put a job off.

The procrastinator tends to put off tasks that must inevitably be dealt with. If you are such a person, you probably waste a lot of precious energy and time in avoiding rather than doing stuff. In the process, you are adding to your stress levels, because certain tasks must eventually be addressed. However, you first need to understand why you tend to procrastinate.

Procrastination often comes from a feeling of hopelessness with regards to a certain situation. You may tend to put off doing something because you have already deemed it as a futile undertaking that is bound to end in failure. Alternatively, you may assume that doing the task serves no purpose, even if your rational mind tells you that it does.

Procrastinators are also unable to accept that someone or something else causes their inability to snap into action. In other words, they do not accept responsibility for their inaction and blame it on outside forces.

The next time you feel like putting off rather than addressing a task, do a quick check of your thought processes. Do you find yourself thinking about all the things that could go wrong with the undertaking? If so, you are setting yourself up for failure with your negativity.

Maybe you approach the situation by making one massive effort to get the task done in one go, and then give up when that doesn't happen. If this is the case, you are only living out a self-fulfilling doom prophecy - many tasks require more dedication to complete, and you are not willing to generate that dedication.

Next, check the words that are running through your mind. Procrastinators engage in a typical kind of self-talk that is replete with the words "I can't," "this is too hard," and so on. There is a marked lack of self-belief. A person who procrastinates on a chronic basis will have labeled himself as a good-for-nothing, powerless, inept and untalented being. He expects very little or nothing from himself, and accepts ineptness and failure as the norm in his life.

There is hope for procrastinators who truly wish to change. Rehabilitation begins with more positive self-talk, in which the procrastinator affirms rather than negates his or her abilities. The mind must be trained to focus on the benefits of seeing a task through rather than focusing on why it cannot be done. It could be as simple as visualizing the freedom of a paid credit card bill, the safety and assurance of undertaking pending repairs on the family car, or the feeling of satisfaction that buying a timely Christmas or birthday gift gives.

## Ways You Can Stop Yourself from Procrastinating:

Is there anything wrong?

If you're not doing something that you know needs to be done, what is the matter and exactly what is stopping you from doing it? The best part about being a procrastinator is that we do not have to face the obstacle that is stopping us from moving forward, as such we need to take control and start eliminating the very thing that is stopping us from getting started.

### Step-by-step plan

If you do not know the power of this already, you should give it a go. Having a step-by-step plan with a deadline can prompt us into action; this also counters the very reason why we procrastinate, which is being overwhelmed by the many things needs to be completed.

### Being Realistic

When you do set up a plan, you need to be realistic in your goal. What I mean is, if your goal is still too big, you will end up not taking action again. It is essential for you to set a realistic goal which you can achieve, this way you will gain the drive to keep going once you've achieved your first goal.

## Get Going

The most effective and easy way to kill off your procrastination habit is doing the exact opposite of it, which is taking action. Taking action, much like procrastinating, is a habit that can be strengthened, the more you practice it, the more likely you are to get into the habit of taking action and stopping procrastinating.

## Taking Scheduled Breaks

When you do schedule your breaks, you will give your body and mind a chance to relax and reenergize itself from the task. This will put you in a better and more productive mindset and lets you get ready to face more challenges. Do make sure that you're not abusing your break by getting back into the procrastination cycle.

Procrastination is simply a habit, one that we must break by taking steps to combat it. Every time you give in to that it's strengthening it, therefore take the steps necessary to weaken it by not giving in and making a choice!

# Chapter 6: How to Be More Productive

I'm pretty sure you might have encountered the feeling of being frustrated with your routine at one point or another. Ever wondered why that happens? I mean no one has forced you to follow it. In fact, you have the sole responsibility of taking that on your own. When you wish to do everything, the only thing that can fail you is improper time management.

The expanding scope of growth makes settling harder and therefore, our greed for achieving more exceeds it and trust me there's nothing wrong with that. In fact, the will to achieve is something that drives us towards success.

When our free mind opens its door to ideas, and we let them settle in, our wish is to grow with them. But while doing this, there comes a stage when the heap of ideas grows too large, and it becomes harder to figure out where to start or more importantly how to do that.

I often struggle with the same problem and get stuck at a point of choosing between these ideas. But facing the situation again and again made me look out for the bigger picture and that's when I understood-

All you need for 100% productivity is a foolproof process.

To get all the right things done at the right time, I've listed out some effective points from my personal experience which are as follows -

**Begin with small things** - Ideas are always useful. No matter how small they are, they demand to be worked upon. Whenever the lightbulb in your mind blinks, make sure you catch the light at the moment itself. Write down your latest ideas or thoughts every day, mind them- every single day.

**Move on step-by-step** - A list is worthless unless it is re-read and revised. Pre-planning is the key here. The list of ideas should be sorted and made ready for application by the end of the day. Once you complete working on your list of today, you can secure your tomorrow for it. Also, if something can be addressed at the moment; there's no harm in it. You have to figure out what fits best for you.

**Do not settle for less** - You might pick only two of the best ideas from yesterday's list but make sure you give your heart and soul to them today. The level of perfection of your mind should match the level of satisfaction of your heart. That's the whole point of successfully moving forward with the plan. Till then just work, work and work.

**Learn time hacks** - When it comes to you, there's no one else to help you organize your time. You need to utilize both hard work and smart work. Consume your energy in a timely manner and give yourself the freedom of short breaks too. Shift on to something interesting during these times like reading, exercise, meditation or anything that is capable of changing your mood. For me of course, writing steals the show.

**Don't kill your creativity** - While doing your job, you might want to dive in with the deepest sincerity, but sometimes when you take all the workload on your shoulders it kills the enthusiasm. There's a solution for this too! Along with your basic work you should also look in for gaps and fill them with your inner creativity. Allow yourself to fit in but don't forget to explore what's outside.

# Chapter 7: Utilizing Habit Pyramids

Humans are said to be 'creatures of habit.' In fact, humans are not alone in exhibiting this interesting form of behavior. Dogs, as well as many other animals, become used to set routines which they assiduously cling to and often grieve for when circumstances change. Why then are these behaviors such an integral part of our lives?

Routines that become habits are a form of mental shortcut we can fall back on in emergencies. On such occasions, the automated response associated with a habit saves time when the time is at a premium. Nowhere does this become more evident when we are engaged in activities such as riding a motorcycle. Riders need to develop a range of automatic responses (habits) which will enable them to make the best use of their machinery in an emergency situation. At such times, a non-automatic response may well have grave consequences.

Habits are the well-worn tracks that govern our daily lives. In these instances, the habits may be a form of mental laziness which obviates the need to think or are used as excuses to evade activities we would rather avoid. We convince ourselves that the importance of performing the routines, the way we do it, is more important. The habits and routines we cling to justify our procrastination and help to satisfy our conscience. The sheer diversity of habits we observe in those around us, suggests that the boundaries and definitions of our lives are bound up with the individual habits that we all perform daily. Routines provide security, certainty, solace and comfort. Daily lives function around the regular activities and habits that people adopt. We are conditioned and programmed to take comfort and pleasure from familiarity.

Conversely, we are encouraged to show caution when tackling the unknown, on the off-chance that unforeseen events may overwhelm us and our coping mechanisms are thrown into turmoil. Habits are part of our mindset, and the sense of security and the feeling that 'all is right with the world' are reasons for resisting change; in that sense, all humans are 'conservative' and addicted to the status quo. We occupy a fundamentally uncaring, seemingly capricious world. Habits act like mantras. These are the mechanisms people use to provide us with a sense of normality, certainty, and acceptance with the world.

Habits can be beneficial as well as damaging, good habits such as those adopted by well-trained motorcyclists can be life-saving. However, bad habits can enslave people and prevent them from reaching their full potential and in fact even be life-threatening. The challenge then is not to live without habits and routines as such, but to focus only on adopting those that are positive.

People may take on a particular habit without thinking through the longer-term consequences, e.g. smoking. The habit appears to be innocuous at the start but has long-term hidden dangers, unknown when the habit was formed. Other such habits could be heavy drinking, eating processed foods, etc. An individual may not abandon such potentially destructive habits until they receive a medical setback by which time, the habit has already caused some damage to the person's health and wellbeing, and is now so ingrained that it is far more difficult to break.

Human history and achievement have been built on the challenges that were met head on, many of our inventions and discoveries that we take for granted, would not be part of our world today if someone hadn't thought 'outside the box,' hadn't broken the habits of tradition and orthodoxy. Habits have their place, but an open mind must be kept if they are not to become the chains that bind us and condemn us to mediocrity.

# Chapter 8: Example - Utilization of Habit Pyramids on Fitness

Personal fitness is to the human body specifically what perfect adjustment is for an engine. This permits all of us to execute up to our probable endurance as well as power. The truth is that personal fitness might be the capability to perform everyday duties intensely as well as alertly, as well as energy staying about having satisfaction in leisure time workouts along with interacting with disaster needs. It is also the chance to withstand, on keeping up, to resist stress and anxiety, to carry on within situations precisely in which an unhealthy individual could not keep on, and it's also a considerable foundation for good health insurance and well-being. Subsequently, it is also concerning your existing emotional stability.

Cutting down weight and turning into a fit and healthy physique is not just done with regards to the bodily element, it's as much about your physique and thoughts. It's necessary for you to take care of all segments of your health and fitness in order to gain that sense of accomplishment. Personal fitness is an individual good quality which differs from one individual to another. Primarily it is counting on older age, genes, personal intercourse patterns, bodily work outs along with eating habits and procedures. Personal fitness needs functionality of the heart, lungs and also muscles for the entire physique to benefit. And also, fitness truly has an effect to some degree on characteristics like emotional performance and psychological stability. Therefore, it's essential for everyone to remain healthy and be in a fantastic physical state to be in a position to utilize personal fitness.

One factor to consider along with physical exercise arrangements, particularly if you are a dyed-in-the-wool non-active, is to discuss your conditions together along with your wellness care distributor. For all those who've difficulties that have completing physical exercises as well as those who find physical fitness a challenge, your wellness treatment provider may suggest you to an exercise physiologist who can pattern a workout program for your specific wants.

Numerous issues associated with particular diseases, may also advise what sort of exercise you might be in a position to consider. Pursuits like excess weight lifting, sprinting, and even high-impact aerobic fitness exercise may not be a good fit for those with diabetic retinopathy, simply because of the danger of a lot more blood vessel injuries in addition to possible retinal detachment. Doctors also claim that sufferers with serious peripheral neuropathy or PN want to prevent exercises which consist of long-distance strolling, operating, or even step aerobics and instead deciding on these with regards to low-impact routines such as going for a swim, or biking, as well as rowing.

For all those who have heart problems, your doctor may want to request you to execute a stress test to determine a wholesome program of fitness for you. If you're currently performing sports activities or get some physical exercise often, it'll eventually be good for you personally to speak about your typical personal routine with your health-related care supplier.

The result is that personal fitness program should be customized to your needs and abilities. Your physical exercise program can be as simple as a nightly stroll within the neighborhood, taking the canine for a stroll, and even basically utilizing the stairs instead of the elevator. The basic aspect is that you proceed to move. Each and every small bit genuinely can help a major amount. In the end, you are going to notice that you will find a lot of advantages that might become as incredibly crucial as personal fitness might be for you.

# Chapter 9: Areas That You Can Apply Positive Habits.

When we ask people what they want in life, they will tell us that they are eager for money, better health, good relationships, a happier family, and wisdom. The answers could be varied, but these five things should be part of the answers.

Why can't we achieve what we dream of when so many success stories have been told to us? People have achieved a high salary income, good relationships with friends and families and better health in life. Unlike them, we are still working harder to get these results. In return, we feel tired of ourselves for achieving nothing.

Our opportunity in life is equal to everyone, but the only thing that differentiates us from the others will be our destiny. Now, how we could change our destiny? The answer is to self-repent. This powerful positive thinking technique is the first thing we should do if we want to change our destiny in life.

We need to go through two processes to self-repent. First, we should sincerely accept the bad consequences that happened to us and stop blaming other people. Next, we stop repeating the same acts in the future. We should keep practicing this powerful positive thinking, even though our determination will be tested when our bad habits come back again. It is the key to bringing luck to our destiny.

The other way to change destiny we should bear in mind is to help those less fortunate. At present, there are a lot of poor and misfortunate people waiting for help from society. Regarding financial help, we could put away some money every month to donate to accredited charity organizations. On the other hand, some people will prefer to become volunteers in some non-government charity organizations. We could choose to join local community programs such as recycling, charity, or free medical checkup activities. At the beginning, we could spend two to three hours a week being a volunteer in those programs.

As we change our destiny, we will need to read positive thinking books or quotes related to self-repenting and good deeds. They will be our guidance which encourages us to stay on path when dealing with daily life difficulties. Soon, if we continue practicing self-repenting and doing good deeds for people, our life destiny will be changed for the better.

Let us share this greatness of positive attitude to more people who want to change their lives for the better.

We are constantly talking to ourselves each day of our lives. This internal voice is speaking to us about ourselves, our friends, neighbors, things and the world at large. Positive self-talk has to be practiced to impact the quality of your life. Every word that we conceptualize within ourselves and utter can be a reflection of our characters. Listening to the inner voice is also referred to as intuition and leads to wise choices.

It is important to understand that positive self-talk directly influences habits, mood, self-esteem, attitude, relations and other facets of individuality. It is a mechanism that works on the repetitive principle where positive information bits are imprinted into the brain to generate positive thoughts. Pay attention to the voices in your head. This will be when that self-sabotage kicks in, trying to remind you why you are not good enough. Remember to say, "Thanks for sharing," and focus back on your personal love fest.

Optimism and motivation are products of a healthy, positive state of mind. These are cultivated by the constant feeding of the self with words of possibility, an enabling environment and lots of motivating words. These work to castigate any negativity that arises from the fear of facing challenges. What we want to manifest with positive self-talk is a belief in our capabilities, and to develop the strength to accomplish anything we set our minds to.

In a scenario of confusion and a life that has no direction, a serious evaluation of perspective needs to take place. You need to incorporate positive self-talk to do away with negativity. Strong or negative words should not be used to break all doubts and uncertainty. The positive words used subconsciously can turn a frustrating situation into a moment of real fulfillment.

People practicing positive self-talk interpret problems differently from negative people. Their differences lie in their interpretation of life problems; positive people distance themselves from adversities and personalize success whereas negative people personalize adversity and distance themselves from success. It determines if self-actualization is achieved and the strongest candidates are the positive people.

Interestingly, any helpful changes in your life come from the belief in all communication to yourself. Your intuition will be able to affirm that you are succeeding in becoming whom you want to be. Posters and other writings can be placed in places frequented regularly to help develop belief and remove all doubt from the consistent and repeated bombardment with positive messages.

Instructions are given to transmit positive self-talk and realize the change in attitude. These include but are not limited to employing the pronoun "I" in all self-talk. Ensure that self-talk remains crisp and potent, and it must be conducted in the present. Be as authentic and reasonable with yourself as possible. Self-talk is to be repeated and can assist in forming habits that make a conversion into a positive state of mind.

# Conclusion

1. Make a "want" list. Whenever you feel like you want to buy something, open up a notepad and write down the good (or service) in question. Come back to it a week later. If you still want to buy the items on the page, go ahead. Don't erase the items that you don't want to buy, however. When you flip through your notepad and see a list of all the stupid crap you thought you wanted, it will inspire you to be more economical. Soon enough, you won't even need the notepad because you will be in total control of your spending. This strengthens your self-discipline, which, in turn, builds your self-confidence.
2. Imagine your life as a timeline. The basics of the technique are as follows: Visualize a timeline in front of you, with giant hovering translucent numbers and any further trappings you desire to cement the image. This timeline represents your life.

    Imagine yourself jumping ahead to sometime in the future; I usually go for two years. Ask your future self if the actions you wish to undertake now will be destructive for your future you. It will always work because on a gut level you already know the correct choice. This is just a way to coax it out of yourself. Say you're in a mall and want to approach an attractive brunette getting a pretzel at Wetzel's, but for some reason, you just can't bring up the nerve to talk to her. Visualize yourself several years in the future and ask, "Will I regret not meeting this fine girl?" If your gut is saying "yes," then you must approach her, for rejection is better than regret.

3. Visual inspiration. Whenever you need strength or inspiration, it's helpful to be able to look to a symbol of your goal. Your goals are more in focus when you have a tangible representation of your aspirations. For example, I like to write inspiring maxims on my cell phone home page. It's dorky, sure, but it works. Every time I'm in need of a boost or feeling uneasy about a situation, I flip open my cell phone and find my visual affirmation.

# The end… almost!

Reviews are not easy to come by.

As an independent author with a tiny marketing budget, I rely on readers, like you, to leave a short review on Amazon.

Even if it's just a sentence or two!

So if you enjoyed the book, please head to the product page, and leave a review as shown below.

I am very appreciative for your review as it truly makes a difference.

Thank you from the bottom of my heart for purchasing this book and reading it to the end.

/

www.ingramcontent.com/pod-product-compliance
Lightning Source LLC
Chambersburg PA
CBHW071038080526
44587CB00015B/2679